Sharks

Hunters of the Deep

by Lola M. Schaefer

Consultant:
Dwight Lawson, Ph.D.
General Curator
Zoo Atlanta

Bridgestone Books
an imprint of Capstone Press
Mankato, Minnesota

Bridgestone Books are published by Capstone Press
151 Good Counsel Drive, P.O. Box 669, Mankato, Minnesota 56002
http://www.capstone-press.com

Library of Congress Cataloging-in-Publication Data
Schaefer, Lola M., 1950–
    Sharks: hunters of the deep/by Lola M. Schaefer.
    p. cm.—(The wild world of animals)
    Includes bibliographical references and index.
    ISBN 0-7368-0828-0
    1. Sharks—Juvenile literature. [1. Sharks.] I. Title. II. Series.
QL638.9 .S265 2001
597.3—dc21
                                                        00-010183

Summary: An introduction to sharks that describes their physical characteristics, habitat, young,
    food, enemies, and relationship to people.

Editorial Credits
Erika Mikkelson, editor; Karen Risch, product planning editor; Linda Clavel, designer and
    illustrator; Kimberly Danger and Heidi Schoof, photo researchers

Photo Credits
Doug Perrine/Innerspace Visions, 12, 16
International Stock/Jeff Rotman, 1
Mark Conlin/Innerspace Visions, 10
Mark Strickland/Innerspace Visions, 18
Norbert Wu/www.norbertwu.com, 14
Photo Network/Hal Beral, 8
Visuals Unlimited/David B. Fleetham, cover, 4, 6, 20

1 2 3 4 5 6 06 05 04 03 02 01

Table of Contents

Sharks

More than 370 kinds of sharks live in the world. Sharks have round bodies that are narrow at each end. Sharks have fins. Fins help a shark swim. Some sharks are smaller than an adult's hand. Other sharks can weigh as much as two elephants.

whale shark

FUN FACTS

The whale shark is the largest living fish. It can grow longer than 50 feet (15 meters) and weigh up to 20 tons (18 metric tons).

What is a Shark?

Sharks are fish. Fish breathe oxygen in the water through gills. Rough scales cover a fish's body. Sharks have tiny, toothlike scales called dermal denticles. Sharks are different from other fish. Most fish have skeletons made of bone. Shark skeletons are made of cartilage.

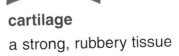

cartilage
a strong, rubbery tissue

white-tipped reef shark

FUN FACTS

Scientists think most sharks live an average of 25 years. But some sharks live to be 100 years old. Scientists also think that sharks have been on Earth for more than 400 million years.

A Shark's Habitat

A shark's habitat is the ocean. Many sharks make their home in warm waters. Other sharks live in icy waters. Some sharks do not travel far from their birthplace. Other sharks swim all over the world.

habitat
the place where an animal lives

silky shark

What Do Sharks Eat?

Sharks eat meat. Sharks that have flat teeth eat crabs and other sea animals that have shells. Sharks break the hard shells with their flat teeth. Sharks that have sharp teeth eat fish, squid, and other sharks. They use their pointed teeth to rip off chunks of flesh.

squid

a sea animal with a long, soft body

sand tiger shark

FUN FACTS

!

Sharks grow new teeth to replace their broken or dull teeth. In its lifetime, a shark may grow 20,000 teeth.

Sharp Senses

Sharks are hunters of the deep. Their senses help them hunt. Sharks can hear sounds and can see well. They also have a good sense of smell. A special sense helps sharks feel the vibrations made by all underwater animals. Sharp senses help sharks survive.

vibrations
fast movements
back and forth

white-tipped reef sharks

FUN FACTS

Male sharks let female sharks know they are ready to mate by nibbling their skin. The scars on the females' skin are known as "love bites."

Mating and Birth

Scientists do not know how sharks mate. Sharks are born in different ways. Some female sharks lay up to 25 eggs in one year. Young sharks hatch from the eggs. Other sharks grow inside their mother's body. Some female sharks can give birth to as many as 100 sharks at one time.

birth of shark pup

Shark Pups

Young sharks are called pups. Adult sharks leave the pups after they are born. Pups know how to swim and hunt. They eat small fish, worms, and shellfish. Shark pups grow slowly. Sharks are not fully grown until they are 10 to 15 years old.

gray reef shark

Enemies

Sharks have few enemies. Large sharks sometimes attack small sharks. People hurt or kill thousands of sharks each year. Sharks are killed for food, oil, skins, and sport. People pollute the air and water. Pollution damages sharks' habitat.

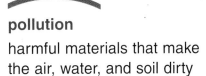

pollution
harmful materials that make the air, water, and soil dirty

scalloped hammerhead shark

Sharks and People

Sharks help people. Sharks help keep oceans clean by eating sick fish. People also try to help sharks. Some people make laws to protect sharks. Sharks often are killed for their meat, teeth, and skin.

Hands On: Why Sharks Swim Easily

A shark stores oil in its liver. The oil-filled liver helps keep the shark from sinking. Try this experiment to see what happens when you mix water and oil.

What You Need

Measuring cups
Salad or cooking oil
Clear container
Water
Food coloring

What To Do

1. Measure one-half cup (125 milliliters) of salad or cooking oil.
2. Pour oil into the clear container.
3. Measure one-half cup (125 milliliters) of water. Add a few drops of food coloring to the water. Mix the water and food coloring together.
4. Pour the colored water into the same clear container as the oil.
5. Watch what happens. The water will sink to the bottom. The oil will float to the top. Oil is lighter than water. Can you see why a shark's oil-filled liver helps keep the shark afloat in the ocean?

Words to Know

cartilage (KAR-tuh-lij)—the strong, rubbery body tissue that makes up most of a shark's skeleton

dermal denticles (DUR-muhl DEN-tuh-kulz)—tiny, toothlike scales that cover a shark's skin

gill (GIL)—an organ on a fish's side; fish breathe with their gills.

liver (LIV-ur)—the body part that stores body oils; the liver cleans the blood.

oxygen (OK-suh-juhn)—a colorless gas found in the air and water

scale (SKALE)—one of the small hard plates that covers the body of a fish or reptile

skeleton (SKEL-uh-tuhn)—the bones that support and protect the body; sharks have cartilage instead of bones.

Read More

Berger, Melvin. *Chomp!: A Book About Sharks.* Hello Reader! New York: Scholastic, 1999.

Holmes, Kevin J. *Sharks.* Animals. Mankato, Minn.: Bridgestone Books, 1998.

Robinson, Claire. *Sharks.* In The Wild. Des Plaines, Ill.: Heinemann Library, 1999.

Internet Sites

All About Sharks
http://www.enchantedlearning.com/subjects/sharks/
Ask Shamu: Sharks
http://www.seaworld.org/ask_shamu/shark.html
Introduction to Sharks
http://www.oceanofk.org/sharks/sharks.html

Index